PROJECTS FOR WINTER

& HOLIDAY ACTIVITIES

Celia McInnes

Illustrated by John Yates

 GARRETT EDUCATIONAL CORPORATION

Projects for Winter

Seasonal Projects

Seasons do not happen at the same time of year everywhere. In the northern and southern halves of the world the seasons are reversed, as this chart shows:

Northern Hemisphere			
Spring	*Summer*	*Autumn*	*Winter*
March	June	September	December
April	July	October	January
May	August	November	February
Autumn	*Winter*	*Spring*	*Summer*
Southern Hemisphere			

©1989 by Garrett Educational Corporation
First published in the United States in 1989 by
Garrett Educational Corporation, 130 East 13th Street,
Ada, OK 74820

First Published in 1988 by Wayland (Publishers) Limited,
England
©1988 Wayland (Publishers) Limited, England

Typset in England
Printed in Italy by Rotolito Lombarda, Milano
Bound in USA

Library of Congress Cataloging-in-Publication Data

McInnes, Celia
    Projects for winter & holiday activities.

    (Seasonal projects)
    Includes index.
    Summary: Presents arts and crafts projects, recipes, games, and
activities associated with the Winter season.
    1. Creative activities and seat work—Juvenile literature. 2. Winter—
Juvenile literature. [1. Handicraft. 2. Winter] I. Yates, John, ill.
II. Title. III. Series.
GV1203.M3564   1989   649.5   88–33515
ISBN 0–9–44483–41–0

Cover/top left *Candles made with colored wax.*
Cover/right *These children have made a snowman*
Cover/bottom left *Making patterns with fruit and
vegetable prints.*

Contents

The seasons happen because every year the earth travels around the sun. The earth is tilted at an angle to the sun, and the part that is nearest the sun is warmer, so it is summer. Later in the year the same part of the earth is tilted away from the sun, so it is winter.

Some parts of the world do not have seasons. At the North and South Poles it is always cold and icy, but at places near the Equator it is always very hot. Countries like Singapore and India have wet and dry seasons instead of summer and winter. In the temperate regions, however, the weather is hotter and the days are longer in summer. In winter it is colder and the days are shorter.

Winter is not the same everywhere. Parts of the USSR, Canada and the United States have very cold winters with heavy falls of snow. In Britain the

Winter weather varies in different parts of the world. In Canada ice skating is a popular winter activity as rivers and lakes freeze over for weeks at a time. These Canadians are skating on a large ice rink in Ottawa, Canada's capital city.

weather is usually much less severe, and in southern Europe it is milder still. In most parts of Australia the winter weather is quite warm.

There are many reasons for the different types of winter weather. It is always colder on high ground, so areas such as the Swiss Alps have more snow. The weather may be milder along the coast of a country. This is because the sea is still warm after the summer. Warm water heats the air above. The air then heats the land when the wind blows from the sea toward the shore.

Wind movement and water currents are affected by the meeting of cold and heat. Try this experiment to see what happens when something cold and something warm come together.

ICE-CUBE EXPERIMENT

Fill a glass bowl or jar with warm water and drop in an ice cube. If you look from the side you will see a swirling movement down from the ice cube as it melts. You will be able to see this better if you make an ice cube with a few drops of food coloring. The movement is the denser icy water sinking through the less dense warmer water in the jar.

MAKE A SNOWSTORM

You will need:
- **a screw-top jar**
- **finely cut silver foil or dried coconut**
- **cake decorations (such as a snowman, robin or fir tree)**
- **water**
- **glue**

1 Open the jar and glue the snowman, robin or fir tree to the inside of the top. Fill the jar with water and add coconut or foil cut into tiny pieces.

2 Screw the top on tightly (make sure it fits properly!) and turn the jar upside down. Shake it and watch the snow fall.

ST. NICHOLAS' DAY

December 6 is known as St. Nicholas' Day in honor of a bishop of Myra (in what is now Turkey) who died on that date in about the year AD 326. St. Nicholas was famous for his love of children and for his generosity.

By the year 1200, the tradition of giving special presents on St. Nicholas' Day was popular in many countries. In the Netherlands these were brought to children by St. Nicholas himself, riding on a white horse, led by Black Peter with his bundle of sticks to punish bad children. The Dutch introduced St. Nicholas into America when they settled here in the seventeenth century.

In the United States the Dutch *Sinter Klaas* gradually became Santa Claus, and merged with the older figure of Father Christmas, but December 6 is still the day when American children write their Christmas letters to Santa. In the Netherlands, Sweden and parts of Austria and Germany, children still wait for St. Nicholas on December 6 and put out hay for his horse.

In the Netherlands people give small presents on this day, often with a short poem, joking about the person receiving the gift. This might refer to his sweet tooth, or to her quick temper. Why not write a poem like this for someone in your family or class? In Germany and Scandinavia, people make gifts from marzipan or gingerbread, often in fancy shapes.

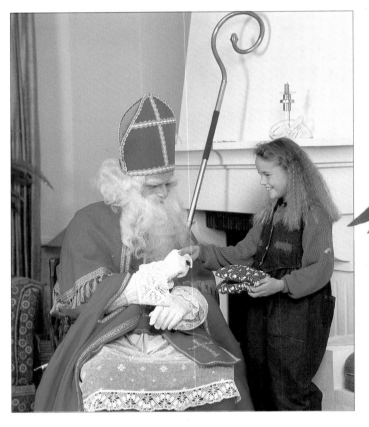

St. Nicholas brings a gift to a German child. This tradition dates from the story of a bishop in the fourth century AD, who was famous for his kindness and love of children.

GINGERBREAD

Use this sweet and spicy gingerbread to make cookies in the shape of the first letters of people's names, or in any other shape you choose.

Safety note:
Be very careful when boiling the mixture, and when taking the cookies out of the oven. Ask an adult to help you.

You will need:

- 2½ oz brown sugar
- 2 tbsp golden syrup
- 1 tbsp molasses
- 1 tbsp cold water
- 1 tsp ginger
- 1 tsp cinnamon
- 3 oz margarine, cut in lumps
- ½ tsp baking soda
- ½ lb white flour

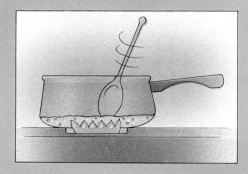

1 Bring the sugar, syrup, molasses, water and spices to a boil, stirring all the time.

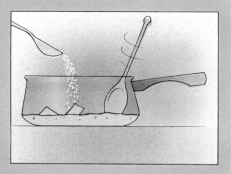

2 Remove from the heat and stir in the margarine and the baking soda.

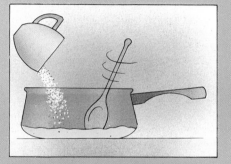

3 Add the flour. Use a little more if the mixture still looks very sticky.

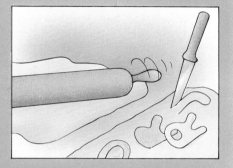

4 Cover and leave for 30 minutes. Turn the oven on to 350°F/180°C and let it heat up.

5 Roll out the mixture about 1/8 in. thick on a floured surface. Cut out letters or shapes, using the point of a knife. You can re-roll any mistakes.

6 Put the cookies on greased baking sheets.

7 Bake for 10 to 15 minutes. Take them out of the oven.

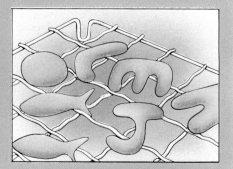

8 Put them on a wire rack to finish cooling. Now they are ready to eat.

HANUKKAH

A Jewish family lighting the eight candles of the menorah on the last night of Hanukkah. This recalls the miracle of a lamp full of holy oil that burned for eight days, 2,000 years ago.

This eight-day festival celebrates the time when, over 2,000 years ago, a rebel group of Jewish warriors defeated the huge army of their Syrian rulers. King Antiochus had forbidden the Jews to practice their religion or to keep their customs, and their temples were closed. It was the village priest, Mattathias, and later his son, Judas Maccabbaeus, who led the Jews to victory.

However, when the Jews came to clean and re-dedicate their temple, they found only one lamp full of holy oil left. It was important to them that a light should burn all the time as a symbol of God's presence, and miraculously the one lamp burned for eight full days until fresh oil could be prepared.

Jews everywhere celebrate this miracle by lighting an eight-branched candelabra called a menorah on the eight days of Hanukkah: one candle the first day, two the second and so on until all are lit on the last night. This is known as the Festival of Lights and the Festival of Dedication, and it is also seen as a festival of freedom.

During Hanukkah, people decorate their homes and hold family parties. They also cook doughnuts or latkes (potato pancakes) in oil, to remember the one container of oil. This is also a time for playing games, and for giving presents. These should be wrapped as prettily as possible, in blue and white, which are the national colors of the State of Israel.

PRINTED WRAPPING PAPER

To make your wrapping paper really special, decorate it yourself. You can make your own patterns with fruit and vegetable prints. Why not make blue and white prints for Hanukkah?

You will need:
- **watercolors or poster paints, mixed fairly thickly**
- **drawing paper**
- **a sharp knife**
- **a small paintbrush**
- **fruits and vegetables**

PRINTS WITH FRUITS AND VEGETABLES

1 Cut your apple, pear, orange, lemon or mushroom in half. Cut the celery or carrots crosswise as shown. Try different ways of cutting to make good shapes for printing.

2 Paint the cut surface evenly. Press this firmly down on the paper and lift carefully to avoid smudging. Cover the whole sheet in this way.

Cover your paper with shapes and patterns like these.

POTATO PRINTS

1 Choose potatoes of a size that you can hold easily in your hand. Scrub them clean.

2 Cut a potato in half and then cut a shape into the flat surface. It is best to stick to a simple shape, but you can use more than one color at a time if you paint them on with care.

3 If you want to change the shape or color you are using, carefully cut a slice of potato off and begin again.

4 Cut out the letters of the alphabet and print them all in blue on white paper, or print the name of the person to whom you are giving the present all over the paper.

Safety note:
You will need quite a sharp knife to cut the fruits and vegetables, so be very careful not to cut yourself. Ask an adult to help you.

WINTER SLEEP

Although nature seems to be sleeping in winter, plants like these winter aconites can push through the frozen earth to bloom.

In winter everything in nature pauses. Plants stop growing, most trees lose their leaves, and the fields look dark and bare. Some birds fly away to warmer climates and many creatures go into hibernation. Bats, mice, ladybugs and frogs are among those that disappear from sight.

However, although the fields look barren, they may be planted with young winter crops, and new buds will have formed on every twig of trees and shrubs. The spears of spring bulbs are already pushing through the frozen earth. The winter world is dormant, waiting for the temperature to rise and the days to get longer for new growth and fresh life to begin.

Today we know that winter comes because our part of the world is at its farthest point from the sun. Many years ago people made up stories to explain the seasons. One of the best known is the Greek myth of Ceres, goddess of crops. This said that when Pluto carried Proserpina away to his kingdom in the underworld, her mother, Ceres, refused to let anything grow on earth until she returned. The other gods said that Proserpina could return as long as she had not eaten anything while in the underworld. Unfortunately, she had eaten six pomegranate seeds, so the gods said that she could return to earth for six months every year, but the other six must be spent with Pluto. While Proserpina was on earth, her happy mother gave it warmth and life, but while she was away Ceres was sad, and winter came to the earth.

CRYSTAL GARDEN

Make a winter garden indoors, full of shape and color. You should be able to buy kits from toy shops.

You will need:
- **water glass (sodium silicate solution)**
- **large glass jar**
- **crystals of copper sulfate (blue), ferrous sulfate (green), nickel sulfate (turquoise), cobalt chloride (dark red), ferric sulfate and zinc chloride (white)**
- **a funnel**

1 Fill the jar almost to the top with the water glass solution. Put it wherever you want to keep it, as it should not be moved once you have added the crystals.

2 Drop in the crystals. Some, such as copper sulfate, come in lumps. Sprinkle the others in, or use a funnel. Try to keep the different crystals separate: the funnel will help.

3 Your crystal garden will soon begin to grow into fantastic shapes: long spidery strands, branching patterns or fluted columns. Each type of crystal will grow a different color, so your garden should be a mixture of blue, green, turquoise, red and white. Some crystals may take longer to grow than others.

Put a lamp behind the crystal garden so that you can see the colors more clearly.

NEW YEAR

All over the world people like to dress up in bright costumes and join in processions to celebrate the New Year.

Nearly all people celebrate the start of their New Year, and it seems they have always done so. The ancient Egyptians, who worked out the first 365-day calendar, held their New Year festivities when the Nile River flooded in September. The Celts' New Year, Samhain (summer's end), fell at the end of October, and Muslims celebrate their New Year eleven days earlier each year, following a lunar calendar that divides the year by the moon.

However, today, as in the past, many varied cultures share similar New Year beliefs and customs. Everywhere it is a time for cleaning and starting afresh. In Japan, *Gan-Tan* is the most important festival of the year, lasting six days from January 1. People pay old debts, settle quarrels and clean their houses.

Another custom, first-footing, is popular in both Vietnam and Britain. People in both countries follow the old belief that the first person to enter the house in the New Year will bring good luck or bad luck to the household in the coming year. In Scotland the first-footer may bring symbolic gifts for good luck: coal for warmth, salt for plenty, or mistletoe for good fortune.

New Year is also a time for fun. All over the world people hold parties, give presents and have parades to celebrate the New Year.

Everywhere, New Year is a time for looking ahead and making resolutions for the year to come. People turn to astrology and almanacs or to old sayings to find out what the future holds for them. There are also many old fortune-telling games.

FORTUNE TELLING

You will need:
- **1 egg**
- **a bowl of cold water**
- **a spoon**

Fill a bowl with cold water. Crack the egg, spoon up a small amount of the white and drop it into the water. See if it makes a shape you recognize – perhaps the first letter of someone's name. People used to do this to find out who they would marry! You can have a lot of fun guessing what the shapes might stand for.

FLOATING FORTUNES

You will need:
- **walnuts**
- **nutcrackers**
- **paper**
- **cocktail sticks**
- **modeling clay**
- **string**
- **a large bowl of water**

1 Halve enough walnuts for everyone present to have one half shell. Take the nuts out of the shells.

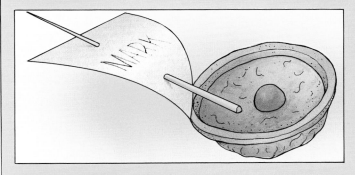

2 Make a tiny sail from a triangle of paper on a piece of cocktail stick. Write your name on the sail and fix it into the nutshell boat with a blob of modeling clay.

3 Write out a number of different fortunes on small pieces of paper, perhaps in rhymes or riddles. Roll these up and tie them with string.

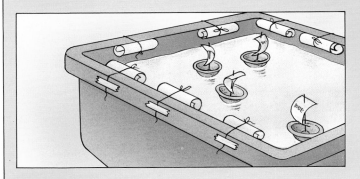

4 Put some water in a large bowl and float the nutshell boats on it. Hang the fortune scrolls over the edge of the bowl.

5 Take turns to blow gently until your boat floats up to a fortune scroll. Then untie the scroll and see what your fortune will be for the year to come!

TWELFTH NIGHT

In Europe, Twelfth Night was traditionally a time for fun and games, marking the end of the Christmas holidays. You can make a wooden board game like this one.

Twelve days after Christmas the three kings from the East – Caspar, Melchior and Balthasar – arrived in Bethlehem to give the baby Jesus their gifts of gold, frankincense and myrrh. This date is known as Twelfth Night, or Epiphany, from the Greek word meaning "the appearance of a divine being." To Orthodox Christians, who have their own calendar, January 6 is Christmas Eve. They also keep January 6 as the day on which Jesus was baptized, and many Greeks hold their children's baptisms on this day.

Today Twelfth Night is a fairly quiet time, marked only by taking down the Christmas decorations, but hundreds of years ago it was a riotous festival with games, feasting, plays and masques. In the streets, workers played practical jokes on passers-by to make the most of the end of the holiday. This Twelfth Night spirit of topsy-turvy fun and tricks lingers on in the French custom of making a *Galette des Rois*, or kings' cake. This is baked with a pea and bean inside. The boy who finds the bean and the girl who finds the pea are king and queen for the day, and everyone should obey them!

The Christmas holiday, which traditionally ended on Twelfth Night, was always a time for families and friends to play games together. Make a wooden board game of zeros and crosses, which is as old as many of these Twelfth Night customs.

ZEROS AND CROSSES

You will need:
- a wood block about 6 in. square, ¾–1 in. thick
- a wooden rod 1 in. thick, 9 in. long
- a hacksaw
- a hand drill
- sandpaper
- varnish or paint

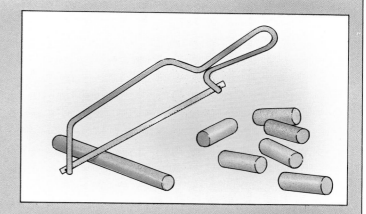

1 Cut the rod into nine pieces, each 1 in. long.

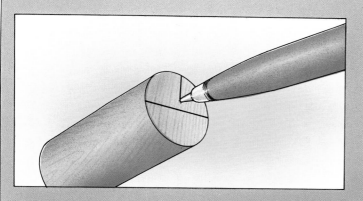

2 Mark one end of each piece with an "O" and the other end with an "X."

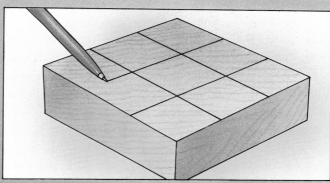

3 Mark the block into nine squares, each 2 in. long.

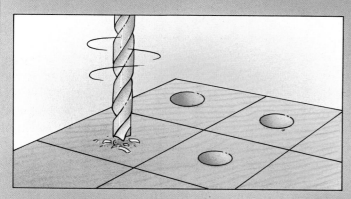

4 Drill a hole in the center of each square, about ½ in. deep. The "O" and "X" pegs will go in these holes.

5 Rub down the wood with sandpaper, and varnish or paint it.
Don't paint over the zeros and crosses!

THE ROMAN CALENDS

Children dressed up for a New Year fancy dress party. In ancient Rome at this time of year, people exchanged their roles in society for the festival of Saturnalia.

It was the Roman Emperor Julius Caesar who set the date of our New Year at January 1 when he introduced his new calendar in 46 BC. This measured the year by the position of the sun, and divided it into the twelve months we know today. In ancient Rome, all public announcements were made on the first day of the month, which was called the "day of proclamation," or in Latin *Calendae*. This is why the New Year celebrations were known as the January *Calends*.

Calends came just after the mid-winter festival *Saturnalia*, when Romans honored Saturn, the god of the harvest. During both festivals there were feasts and games. Gifts of honey or fruit decorated with gold and silver were given to friends and to the emperor. The rules of society were relaxed for a time, or even turned upside down, so that slaves changed places with their masters. This may be why people today dress up to play different roles at New Year fancy dress parties.

PERPETUAL CALENDAR

The word calendar also comes from the Latin *Calendae*. Most people now use the Gregorian calendar, which was adjusted from Julius Caesar's version by Pope Gregory in 1582. This changes slightly every year, so that the first day of a month might fall on a Monday one year, Tuesday the next and so on. However, this perpetual calendar can be used every year, and is easy to make.

You will need:
- **firm cardboard**
- **scissors**
- **compasses**
- **a paper fastener**
- **colored pens**

1 Cut two circles of cardboard about 9 in. in diameter.

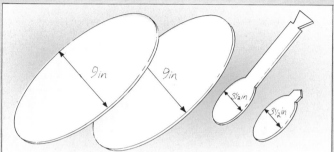

2 Cut out two more circles about 3½ in. in diameter, leaving an arm on each, as shown. One arm should reach beyond the outer edge of the calendar, so it should be longer than 4½ in. from the center of the circle to the end of the arm. The other arm should be about 3 in. long from the center.

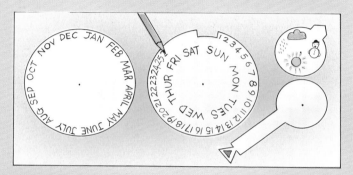

3 Mark the circles as shown. On the week and day circle, allow 34 spaces around the edge. Write down 1 to 31 for the days of the month, and cut a window of 3 spaces so that the month of the year will show through.

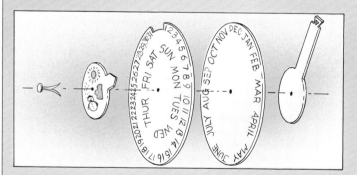

4 Put the calendar together as shown, with the day arm on top, then the week circle, then the month circle, and finally the date arm. Fasten them all together with a paper fastener.

5 You can decorate the calendar with pictures of the seasons. Set it to the right day, date and month. All you have to do now is remember to turn it one space every day.

Snow can bring great hardship to animals like this fox; yet others burrow inside the snow to protect themselves from the cold air.

In some parts of the world, winter brings snow. Although people may not look forward to the cold of winter, most of them enjoy the first fall of snow.

Each snowflake is made up of a cluster of crystals. These are formed when the cold causes water vapor to freeze around a central point. Snow crystals have six points branching out from the center, but always in a different pattern: every single one is unique.

As well as being pretty to look at, snow serves a useful purpose, as an insulator. The snow works like a baby's blanket: the still air trapped inside every crystal prevents frosty air from getting through to the ground and damaging plant shoots and seeds. This is why some animals dig their winter homes in deep snow to keep warm.

Snow does not always come with the lowest temperatures. You can sometimes see hibernating animals such as groundhogs and squirrels popping out while snow is on the ground, to have a quick search for food before returning to hibernation.

However, for those animals that are not tucked away for the winter, snow can bring great hardship, as it covers up their food supplies. If the snow freezes, animals cannot dig through it to get to their food. Frozen ponds and puddles mean no drinking water, and fish in ponds have no oxygen to breathe if the pond is iced solid. For birds especially, winter can be a very hard time.

BIRD BELL

Help the birds in your area to survive the winter with this feeding bell.

You will need:
- **a plastic cup**
- **fine string**
- **a darning needle**
- **a matchstick**
- **food**
- **grease left over from cooking**
- **modeling clay**

1 Thread string through the base of the cup as shown, holding it in place with a matchstick.

2 Stir up a mixture of dried fruit, bread and household scraps such as bacon, cooked potato, cheese and oatmeal.

3 Plug the base hole with modeling clay, and fill the pot with the food.

4 Heat the grease in a saucepan to melt it, but don't let it get too hot as this will melt the cup.

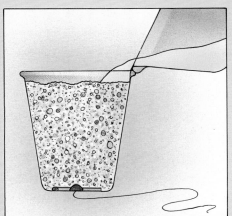

5 Pour in the melted grease, and leave it to set. Wait until it is cool and hard.

6 Hang the bell upside down from a branch or balcony. Make sure it is somewhere that cats cannot reach.

Safety note:
Be very careful when heating the grease as this can be dangerous. Ask an adult to help you.

Draw pictures of the birds that come to your feeding bell and look up their names in a book. Write down which types you see and when you see them. As the weather gets warmer you will find that some birds are leaving and different ones are taking their place.

CHINESE NEW YEAR

Most people are aware of the Chinese New Year celebrations because of the lively dragon processions that take place wherever the Chinese live. However, the dragon is only part of the festival.

The Chinese New Year is a time for starting anew, so homes are cleaned, new clothes bought, and old debts paid. Families want Tsao Chun, the god who watches over the home, to give a good report of them when he visits heaven at the end of the year.

Everything possible is done to keep in good luck and chase away evil spirits. Good luck mottoes on lucky red paper are stuck on doors, and children receive gifts of money in red envelopes. When the families sit down to their New Year feast, they seal the doors with red paper to keep out evil spirits.

The celebrations continue for two weeks with the Feast of Lanterns, when homes are hung with lanterns that symbolize the return of warmth and light after the winter. Then there are the famous

The dragon dance for the Chinese New Year celebrations in Hong Kong. The dragon winds its way through the streets to bring strength and good luck to everyone for the year ahead.

dragon processions. One of the greatest of these is in the Chinatown section of San Francisco. Here there are dozens of floats, and the sound of gongs, cymbals and firecrackers to frighten off bad spirits. The dragon stands for strength and good luck, and is made up of a beautiful framework with 50 or so men underneath to support it as it twists and turns through the streets.

The Chinese also celebrate their birthdays on New Year's Day. At the same time they remember those who have died, and burn paper play money as an offering to their ancestors in heaven.

YOUR FAMILY STORY

The Chinese have great respect for their ancestors. You may be surprised to see how interesting it can be to find out about yours and to draw your own family tree.

Ask people in your family to tell you about the earliest ancestor whose full name and date of birth are known. You can then ask at the city hall or courthouse for this person's birth certificate. This will tell you the full names of the person's parents, their dates of birth, and other details that will help you to carry on working your way back. Look at old photograph albums, and documents too. Older members of the family can be very helpful, and will probably enjoy the chance to tell you what they remember. Their memories are a living link with the past.

Your family tree may not go back very far, or it may have many gaps. However, you can use what you know to write down your family story, from the earliest records you have found to the present day. Write down where the people lived, what jobs they did, and the stories about them that you find the most interesting. Use photographs or draw your own pictures to go with the story.

Talking to older relatives can teach you a lot about your family's past. Ask to look at any photographs or documents that will tell you more.

Now you can start to write down your family story. Put any pictures you are allowed to borrow in a scrapbook to illustrate the story.

BASANT

Sikhs calculate the date for their festivals by the lunar calendar, which means that each month is the time between two new moons, so they fall on different dates from year to year. The festival of Basant, shared by Sikhs and Hindus, falls in either January or February and celebrates the coming of spring. Basant is marked by special services at the temple, and by lots of fun as families get together for the occasion. It is also felt to be a good day for little children to start school.

Yellow, the color of spring in India, is the main color of Basant. People make an effort to wear yellow clothes and cook yellow rice for their meals.

In many towns and villages of India, Basant is a time for kite-flying competitions. A simple kite is not at all difficult to make — you could even make a yellow one for Basant.

You can make this basket and heart-shaped candies as a Valentine gift.

MAKING A KITE

You will need:
- **thin wooden rod or split cane**
- **plastic sheeting or stiff paper**
- **strong thread or string**
- **sticky tape**

Safety note:
Be very careful when cutting the wood to make the frame of the kite, as you will need quite a sharp knife.

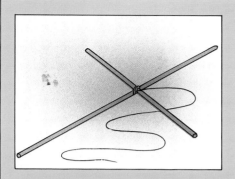

1 Cut the wood in two pieces so that one piece is about 24 in., the other 16 in. long. Lay the short stick across the long stick above its middle, and tie them together with string.

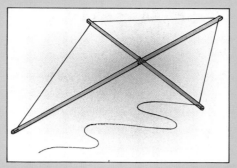

2 Cut notches in the ends of the wood. Tie string to the end of one of the sticks, and stretch it around the frame, through the notches as shown.

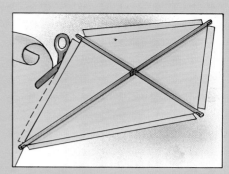

3 Put the frame onto a piece of paper or plastic, and cut around it in a kite shape, leaving about 1 in. all the way around the frame.

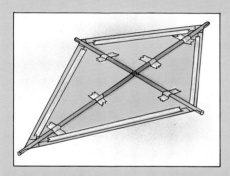

4 Using sticky tape, attach the paper or plastic to the frame. Fold over the edges and stick them down.

5 Make a tail by tying twists of paper to a length of thread or string about 1 or 2 yd. long. If you are using plastic, cut a strip about 1 yd. long and tie it to the kite.

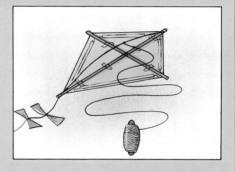

6 Tie another piece of thread to the top and bottom of the long stick. Tie the long kite line to this loop, about a third of the way down.

In many countries, kite-flying is a popular pastime. You may need a little practice before you get things right. Experiment with the length of tail, where you attach the kite line, and even with the shape of the kite. As long as the kite presents a constant flat surface to the wind, it can be any shape you like.

It is said that in the third century BC a Chinese leader used kites to help him to win a battle. He attached special strings to the kites and flew them over the enemy camp. The strings vibrated in the wind and made an eerie sort of music. The enemy thought that this was the wailing of their ancestors, telling them to flee — so they did!

To make your own "buzzer," cut a fringe in a piece of paper and stick it to the loop of your kite.

WINTER LIGHT

Today electric light is available to most people at the flick of a switch, and we do not always realize the importance of the sun and daylight to our ancestors. However, we still look forward to the return of the longer days after the winter. February 2 was the old Celtic festival of Imbolc, which celebrated their return. In the Christian calendar, it is Candlemas, the "Feast of Candles." This recalls the purification of Mary after the birth of Jesus, and the time when Jesus was first presented to the priests at the temple. Christians light candles at church services, or have them blessed by a priest, and take them home as charms against evil. Candles can be seen as symbols of Jesus as the light of the world, and of our earthly daylight.

Buddhists all over the world light candles in their temples on the day of the February full moon. This is for Magha Puja — a Puja is an act of worship, and this one commemorates events in the life of the Buddha. To Buddhists the light of candles symbolizes life, truth, and the triumph of good over evil.

MAKING CANDLES

You will need:
- **candle wax granules**
- **stearin (a hardener) in a disk, with dye added**
- **a length of wick or soft string**
- **a mold**
- **an old saucepan**
- **a pencil**

Those items that cannot be found in the kitchen can be bought at craft suppliers. Use the base of a clean plastic bottle or a plastic cup as a mold, depending on the size and shape of candle you want to make.

If you have a some old wax crayon stubs, melt them down with the wax granules.

Safety note:
Be careful when heating the wax. Ask an adult to help you.

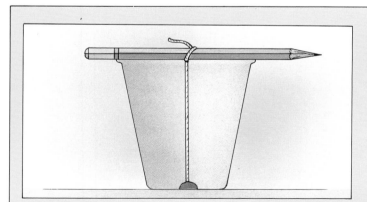

1 Tie a length of wick to a pencil and rest this on your mold so that the wick falls to its base. Stick the wick to the base of the mold with a blob of melted wax.

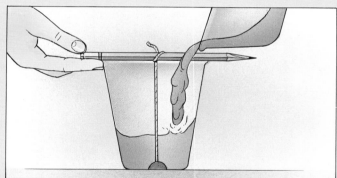

2 Melt the wax in the saucepan. If you are using granules, add 1 part stearin to 9 parts wax. Pour into the mold. Hold the pencil as you do this, and be careful not to let the wax drip onto your hand.

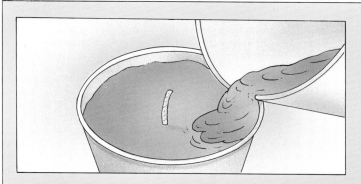

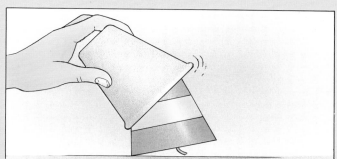

3 Leave to cool, but don't chill. The wax will shrink slightly as it sets, so add a little more every so often to keep the top of the candle level.

4 Take the candle out of the mold. If it will not come out easily, chill it for half an hour and try again.

If you want to give your candle as a present, make it in a sundae or wine glass instead of a mold. Hang the wick in the glass, and allow the wax to cool a little before pouring it in, so that it does not crack the glass.

If you use more than one color of wax, you can either leave one layer to harden before adding the next, or stir them gently together for a marbled effect.

DECORATE A PLAIN CANDLE USING CRAYONS

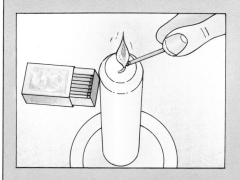

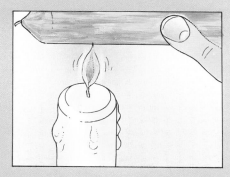

1 Stand a candle firmly upright, and light it. Always be very careful when using matches and working with flames. Ask an adult to help you.

2 Take another candle to decorate. Soften the ends of the crayons in the candle flame and dab onto the other candle until it is covered with colored dots.

3 Hold the dotted candle horizontally over the flame and turn it so that the colors melt and run together. Don't keep it still for too long, or the candle itself will melt.

ST. VALENTINE'S DAY

Our present-day Valentine customs come from a mixture of pagan and Christian tradition and ancient folk beliefs. St. Valentine was probably a priest killed on February 14 in the time of the Roman Emperor Claudius in the third century AD. He became known as the saint of lovers because he performed forbidden marriage ceremonies for Roman soldiers. They were not supposed to marry because it made them less able to fight.

However, February 14 had already been celebrated for centuries by the Romans as *Lupercalia*. This was a fertility festival when young people drew lots to find a partner. The early Christian Church used the tradition of St. Valentine to adopt the pagan feast of *Lupercalia* and give it Christian meaning.

Falling as it does in late winter, February 14 was also believed to be the day the birds chose their mates – in fact, Valentine's Day has become a celebration of anything to do with love.

The early love lotteries led to the tradition of Valentine cards being anonymous; just as young Romans did not know which partner they were choosing, so today people do not know who has sent them a card.

In the past, anonymous gifts were also sent, and in some parts of Britain, special Valentine buns were baked.

You can make this basket and heart-shaped candies as a Valentine gift.

Today Valentine's Day is an excuse for any sort of romantic celebration or exchange – a chance to let someone know you are interested in them, or for a secret admirer to declare his or her love to you.

HEART-SHAPED BASKET

Make a Valentine basket filled with heart-shaped candies for a friend, or for someone you love.

You will need:
- **pink and white paper**
- **pencil and ruler**
- **scissors**
- **stapler**

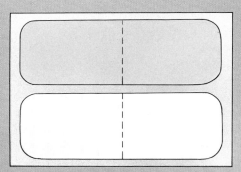

1 Cut a strip 3 in. x 9 in. from each color paper and fold in half. Cut around the outer ends as shown.

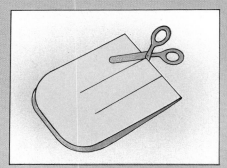

2 Cut twice up the paper from the fold for about 3 in.

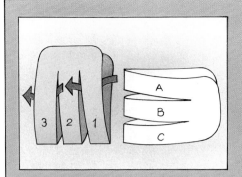

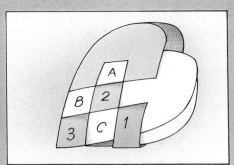

3 Lay both strips at right angles as shown. Push A through loop 1, then push loop 2 down through A. Now tuck A inside loop 3.

4 Now push loop 1 down through B, and push B through loop 2. Then tuck loop 3 inside B. Now weave in C following the same steps as for A.

5 Staple on a paper handle. Now you can make peppermint creams to go in your heart-shaped Valentine basket.

PEPPERMINT CREAMS

You will need:
- **1 egg white to every 10½ oz icing sugar**
- **peppermint essence**

1 Beat the egg white until it is stiff, and add sieved icing sugar.

2 Add peppermint essence, or any other flavor you like.

3 Mix to a stiff paste and roll out on a surface dusted with icing sugar.

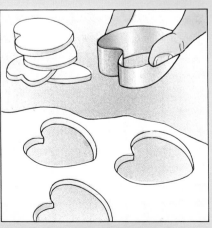

4 Cut out heart shapes and leave sweets to set.

SHROVE TUESDAY

The Mardi Gras festival in New Orleans, Louisiana.

In the Christian calendar, Shrove Tuesday is the last day before Lent begins. Lent was traditionally a time of fasting in memory of Jesus' forty days in the wilderness. Christians would not eat eggs, fat or meat at this time, so any of these left after the winter were finished up on Collop Monday (when collops, or slices of bacon and eggs, were eaten) and on Shrove Tuesday, in pancakes.

The name Shrove Tuesday arose because people went to church to be shriven (forgiven their sins) on that day.

Shrovetide was traditionally a time for letting off steam before Lent, when all fun and feasting were forbidden. There were pancake races, where people had to run while tossing a pancake, and an early type of soccer match, in which hundreds took part. A ball of wood or cork, or a bladder filled with water was kicked up and down the village for up to two days, and goals were often scored in ponds or streams. These traditions are still carried on in some parts of Britain and in the United States.

In New Orleans, Shrove Tuesday is known as Mardi Gras, which is French for fat, or greasy, Tuesday. This is the final day of a spectacular festival in which the streets are full of people in fancy dress and parades of decorated floats. The famous carnivals of Trinidad and Rio de Janeiro also began as celebrations before the beginning of Lent: the word carnival comes from the Latin *carnem vale*, which means "farewell to meat."

In France Mardi Gras is also a time for processions and fireworks, and in the south there are flower festivals like the famous one in Nice. There may not be many flowers out yet where you live, but you can make some to pretend that spring is on its way.

You will need:
- **cotton ball**
- **crepe or tissue paper**
- **pipe cleaners**
- **scraps of cloth**
- **cotton thread**
- **sticky tape**

PAPER FLOWERS

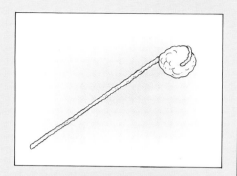

1 Bend the end of a pipe cleaner into a hook. Tuck a small ball of cotton into the hook.

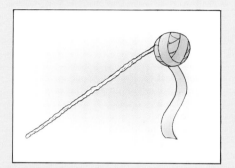

2 Attach a strip of cloth or tape to the hook, and wind it around to cover the ball of cotton. If you use cloth, fix the end to the pipe cleaner with thread. This makes the center of the flower.

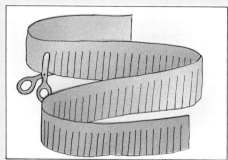

3 Cut a length of paper. Make a fringe by cutting across the grain about every 1/8 in. Cut three-quarters of the way down the paper, as shown.

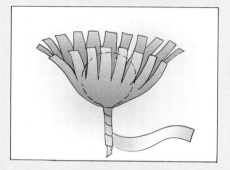

4 Wind the uncut end of the fringe around the center of the flower, and fix it to the stem with tape.

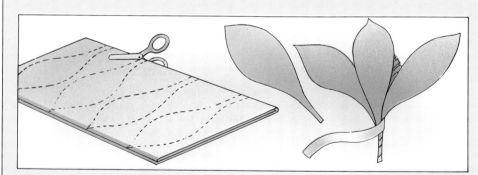

5 Cut out petals from the paper, in any shape or color you like. You can fold the paper and cut lots together for speed. Fix them to the stem with tape, one at a time so they overlap. If you use crepe paper, you can stretch some of the petals to vary their shape and make them curve out at the top, like real flowers.

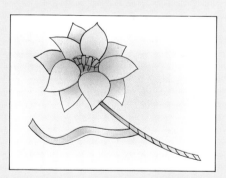

6 When you have enough petals, wind some more crepe paper around the stem and fix with tape, so that no loose ends are showing.

Glossary

Almanac A calendar that tells you the dates of festivals and public holidays, and makes predictions for the year ahead.

Ancestor Someone related to you who lived long ago.

Anonymous Something with no name on it, such as a poem, painting, card or gift.

Astrology The study of the influence the stars are supposed to have on the lives of people.

Baptism A religious ceremony in which a child is thought to be cleansed of sin and welcomed into the Christian Church.

Dedicate To set a place aside for religious purposes.

Equator An imaginary line around the middle of the earth, half way between the North and South Poles.

Hibernation Spending the winter hiding away asleep. Many animals in cold climates hibernate when food is scarce during the winter.

Masque A type of play with singing, dancing and disguises. They were popular at the English court in the sixteenth and seventeenth centuries.

Mottoes Short sayings.

Orthodox Christians Members of a branch of the Christian Church that covers much of eastern Europe, including Greece and Russia.

Pagan Related to a pre-Christian religion such as those of ancient Greece and Rome.

Pomegranate A fruit that has many seeds and flesh that you can eat.

Temperate regions The parts of the earth between the Tropic of Cancer and the Arctic Circle in the northern hemisphere, and the Tropic of Capricorn and the Antarctic Circle in the southern hemisphere.

Tropics The tropics are found between the Tropic of Cancer and the Tropic of Capricorn – two imaginary lines that are at equal distances north and south of the Equator. The tropics have a very hot, and often very wet, climate.

Underworld In Greek mythology this was where the spirits of the dead lived.

Picture acknowledgments

Canada House, London 4; Chapel Studios 9, 14, 21 (both), 26, cover (bottom left); Bruce Coleman Ltd 10 (Jane Burton), 18 (Jane Burton); Chris Fairclough cover (right); Hong Kong Tourist Association 20; Ann and Bury Peerless 22; Zefa 6, 8, 12, 16, 28.

Index